Leaders Who Worship

Worshippers Who Lead

A Beginner's Guide

By Avari Gammage

Cover Design: Shorne Callahan
Editor: NJ Kingdom Enterprises, LLC.
www.njkingdomenterprises.com

I dedicate this book to myself.
Girl, you Finished! (Well, really started, lol).
You made a commitment to yourself and God
that we would finish. I am proud of you! Step
into and remember Jeremiah 29:11

Acknowledgment

I would like to acknowledge my Lord and Savior, Jesus Christ, for without Him, none of this would be possible. I am grateful for the trust He has placed in me to speak to worship leaders around the world and for gifting me beyond what I could naturally see.

I also acknowledge my family, my husband, and my children for their continual support, prayers, and love.

I am thankful for those who have paved the way for me to be who I am today. A special thank you to those who have spoken into my life, prayed over me, given me sound wisdom and advice, and loved me through my journey.

Lastly, my heartfelt appreciation goes to my pastors, Pastor Powe, Pastor Deborah, Pastor Bryan, and Pastor Rashida, and all the leaders, family, and friends of Revealing Truth Ministries.

Table of Contents

Introduction

Do you know why you've been called? Have you ever been given an assignment that seemed over your head? Have you ever been put in a position that made you feel inadequate? Have you ever been put in an environment where you've been asked to expand but not sure how to start? Have you ever felt unqualified but knew something in you was pulling you forward? I know exactly how you feel! I've felt it all!

When I first got the assignment as a worship leader, I didn't feel prepared at all. It felt like I was in over my head. I was not clear about the why, and I did not even really understand the purpose, but I knew I felt God. I knew God was calling me from the inside out. I knew it was something He was calling me to do and not myself.

With this book, I have been entrusted with the significant responsibility of creating a comprehensive guide tailored specifically for worship leaders, particularly those new to the role or lacking formal training. My primary objective is to equip individuals in this capacity with practical and spiritual tools that can effectively support and enhance their leadership.

Drawing from my extensive 14-year journey as a worship leader, I have gained invaluable insights and experiences that I am passionate about sharing to assist others who may be encountering obstacles or feeling isolated in their own paths. Recognizing the profound and demanding responsibility that comes with being a worship leader, I am committed to offering reassurance and guidance to those who may be grappling with the weight of their role.

My ultimate goal is to provide mentorship and a platform for individuals to glean from my experiences, empowering them to transcend their current challenges. I am driven by the aspiration to extend guidance, unwavering support, and the prospect of a new direction for anyone seeking assistance.

I firmly believe that by openly sharing my personal journey, I can provide substantial and meaningful aid to those who find themselves in the midst of the journey. I believe sharing my story and the ways God prepared me for leading worship and becoming a worship pastor will encourage others to see how God is at work in their own lives.

Who is Avari?

I was born and raised in beautiful Tampa, Florida, and lived a simple life centered around God, family, music, and church. My family was very musical, and the love for music and God's presence was deeply ingrained in our daily lives. From attending church regularly to singing on the spot at family functions to praying in the mornings before going to school, our lives were God and music-centered. Although singing came naturally to me, I was very nervous to perform in front of others due to being an introvert. However, behind closed doors, I had undeniable encounters with God from a young age, including speaking in tongues at age nine and receiving visions of people to pray for whom I had never met.

One significant moment that shaped my life was when I first read Jeremiah 29:11. This scripture, read in my room next to my stuffed animals, made me realize that my life was not my own and that there was a greater purpose for me. This understanding led me to discover my calling over time. As I continued to grow in my faith, I had diverse experiences that seemed unrelated initially but later became essential for my leadership development. This journey began when I started working at our church academy and preschool. Starting as an assistant teacher, I learned the values of sacrifice and submission to authority. Despite being capable of running a classroom independently, I understood the importance of working under the lead authority's direction. This experience eventually led to me becoming a lead teacher. I realized that God had been shaping and equipping me for this all along. It was such a comforting realization that God had been preparing and positioning me for this role. He had been giving me all the necessary tools to step into this next chapter of my life. It's amazing how God works behind the scenes to prepare us for what's ahead!

I remember a time when I served as a youth leader under my Youth Pastor, Adrian McCray. He taught me that serving was about meeting the needs of people and becoming all things to win some. In my time serving with him, I watched his character, his patience, and his ability to love people right where they were. I watched him loving the unlovable, helping those who others rejected to see God for themselves, serving families, and serving through Grace. He taught me leadership skills that later in life helped me become who I am today.

I also recall that during this time, I was a freshman college student studying to be a pediatrician. One day in my English class, I heard the voice of God say, "I need your voice." I immediately questioned myself, saying, "Me?! How? I don't want to sing, I don't want to be in front of people, I don't have the confidence." Then, I recalled a worship encounter where I prayed for the people of my church. The Lord reminded me of what I said during that prayer: "God, I want to be used by you to bring peace to people." At the time of that prayer, I didn't know exactly how I wanted to be used, but I knew that I wanted God to be glorified in my life. I left the classroom and continued on with my life.

Not even a few weeks later, I got called into the office after service on a Sunday and was asked to be the worship leader of my church. I had no skills, no resume, and no interview - just a heart to serve. I was shocked, stunned, and quite frankly scared, but I knew it was God. I knew it was God calling me to a higher place. Looking back, I can see what God was preparing me for through the areas in which I served. It was uncharted territory for me, but it was exciting. The journey had begun.

I started my first week as the worship pastor. Now, mind you, I'm the first-ever worship pastor hired as a staff member in the history of my ministry. Talk about nervousness! However, one day, I met a man named Brother Bill, who taught me another tool of my toolbox. Brother Bill, at the time, was our minister of music. He was an older gentleman with a giddy laugh and a huge heart. He taught me the key to becoming a great leader is to prioritize God above everything else. Before making a plan, creating a song list, or speaking to people, I prioritize spending time with God daily. I set aside 30 minutes to an hour for worship. I shared a space with the music director. During that time, I would lock myself in the room, sometimes lie on the floor, and pray in tongues until I heard something from God. I would lose myself in His presence, quieting the noise and focusing on Him. I was desperate. I had never led worship before or led people in this capacity before, but I knew I needed God's instructions to accomplish what He desired. Those quiet times became the lifeline of my Ministry. There, I received strategies, plans, guidelines, and daily instructions from God for myself and those I was called to serve. Seeing how God led and guided me through the Holy Spirit for vision was amazing.

You're probably wondering, Avari, why are you telling me your life story? Get to the good stuff. Well, if you don't first take the time to reflect on your life, you'll easily feel unqualified to walk in the role of Worship leader or Worship Pastor. **Reflecting** is important to help you see how God has been preparing you for your assignment. It puts you in a good starting position of humility and thanksgiving, which you should always return to throughout your journey of becoming a Leader who Worships and Worshipper who Leads!

Pause Moment:

What moments in your life do you believe prepared you for your leadership role? Reflect and Write your response:

_____

_____

_____

_____

_____

_____

_____

_____

_____

_____

_____

_____

_____

Chapter 1 - Where Do I Start?

In my quiet time with the Lord, locked in my office space, I asked God how to understand the role of a worship leader/pastor. The first thing I felt from God was not to allow the title of worship leader or pastor to take me away from just being a worshipper. That is who I am at the core. We must recognize that we have all been called to worship. He wants our devoted attention. Understanding our assignment of living in worship is essential.

What is worship? Is it singing, dancing, or playing instruments, or is it in the lights, a moment, or an experience? I contend that, at its core, **Worship is a Lifestyle**. It's the submission of our will and hearts to God. My pastor says it this way, " Worship is not just the lifting of the hands, but it's the submission of the heart." The word "worship" in the dictionary means to honor or show reverence for a divine being or supernatural power, or to regard with great or extravagant respect, honor, or devotion. This is very true. The Bible shows us in several places that we are to honor the Lord, to show reverence. We honor Him through our giving and our bodies.

Proverbs 3:9 says to honor the Lord with your substance, and 1 Corinthians 6:20 encourages us to use our bodies to honor God. Romans 12:1 in the Amplified Bible says, "Therefore, I urge you, brothers and sisters, by the mercies of God to present your bodies, dedicating all of yourselves set apart as a Living Sacrifice holy and well-pleasing to God, which is your rational, logical, intelligent act of worship. (KJV)

Worship is a lifestyle. God is looking for you, not a title. That is not to diminish the weight of the responsibility, but it is to keep the balance of your heart towards him first. In this journey, people will have expectations of you because of the title, and they should. Knowing who you are at the core will keep you humble, focused and appreciative.

Pause Moment:

Who has God said that you are at the core?

_____

_____

_____

_____

_____

_____

_____

_____

_____

_____

_____

_____

_____

Chapter 2 - Worship is a Lifestyle

Romans, Chapter 12 talks about us presenting our bodies to God as our act of worship. It's our everyday walking-around lives that become our daily worship. It's us acknowledging God's presence in our lives before every decision, before every reaction, before every response.

In scriptures, Jesus oftentimes spoke of this daily walk of worship. For example, in John 2:49, Jesus says "I don't speak on my own authority. The Father who sent me has commanded me what to say and how to say it." (KJV)

Here Jesus is demonstrating his trust in God and not himself. Worship is the submission of your authority to a higher authority. It's the statement of "Not my will but let Your will be done." We must daily practice a lifestyle of worship. As stated in the earlier chapters, when I had those quiet moments of

11

prayer, the Lord began to show me ways to worship as a life-style. I began asking God about everything from the smallest thing to the biggest, such as, Lord, what should I wear today? Which road should I take to work today? Should I respond to this text? Do I email this person, etc.? It was me making a conscious decision to acknowledge God's voice before mine. It was me consciously choosing to align my will with His will. It's a constant exchange.

God took me to the scripture, Proverbs 16:39 (AMP) which says, "Roll your works upon the Lord, commit and trust them wholly to Him, and He will cause your thoughts to become agreeable to His will and so shall your plans be established and succeed." The Message translation says to put God in charge of your work, and then what you've planned will take place." (MSG)

Imagine living your life by first acknowledging God in every moment. It takes patience, humility, and trust to live this life-style. Worship, at its core, is an expression of reverence and adoration. It's about recognizing the divine in our midst and responding with our whole being. This understanding invites us to expand our view of worship beyond the walls of a church or the confines of a prayer mat. Worship is not merely a series of acts but a continuous posture of the heart.

Living the life of worship can then translate into worship's expression. Not having a lifestyle of worship can limit worship's expression. This principle is foundational: to lead effectively, worship must become our lifestyle!

Pause Moment:

In what areas in your life have you acknowledged God, and in what areas have you not acknowledged God?

_____

_____

_____

_____

_____

_____

_____

_____

_____

_____

_____

_____

_____

_____

The Transformative Power of Worship

The presence of God is transformative. It's the secret place where we find refuge, strength, and guidance. Psalm 91 encapsulates this beautifully:

"He that dwelleth in the secret place of the most High shall abide under the shadow of the Almighty. I will say of the Lord, He is my refuge and my fortress: my God; in him will I trust." Psa. 91:1 (NKJV)

To dwell is to live in his presence continuously; to abide is to remain stable and fixed in this divine relationship; in other words- Intimacy. Worship is not confined to songs. It's a way of being a continuous offering of our lives to the divine. **When we embrace worship as a lifestyle, every moment becomes an opportunity to connect with the sacred. Our hearts open, our spirits lift, and our lives transform.**

Leading from a place of personal experience and intimacy with God is vital because we cannot guide others to a place we have not been. Jesus often set examples for this, as seen in John 13 where He states, *"I go to prepare a place for you, and when everything is ready, I will come and get you."* (NKJV) He also emphasized this in Hebrews 4, where He talks about being a High Priest who understands our weaknesses because He faced them all. Just as Jesus led the people through his own experience and intimacy with God, we as leaders must do the same. It's one thing to hear about it, but another thing to experience it for yourself. It's like giving this great description of a trip to Disneyland in California. You describe to the person all the rides, what it looks like, and the different attractions, and the person asks have you ever been and you say, "No, I just read it online, or someone else told me about it."… huh?! **With no direct experience, there can't be a confident transformation**. There is no way for you to speak confidently about the presence of God and the kingdom of God without experience in His presence and His word. This means that our public worship must stem from our private devotion.

Foundational Truth:

You can't expect people to go where you have not been.

The Stage Reflects Your Life

So, how does the worship lifestyle show up in the corporate worship experience? The answer is simple: **The stage is a direct reflection of your life.** It's a platform where authenticity matters. It doesn't matter what you sing about on stage if it doesn't reflect the life you live daily. Using the platform as a practice, we lead from where we are and what we know. When we lead, our prayer and focus should be that people trust the

Holy Spirit as He guides them to the throne of grace (Hebrews 4:16). This means leading them to lay down their cares and hear God's promises. It starts with us being willing vessels, familiar with the secret place of God's presence. As Psalm 91 stated, dwelling and abiding in that place makes us His mouthpiece, connecting people to victory and serving as conduits for the Holy Spirit.

> ### Foundational Truth:
> **Authenticity Matters!**

Worship is unconditional because we serve an unconditional God. It's an altar, a place of sacrifice, meaning it's not predicated on conditions. God tells us to worship in season and out of season. It's about understanding the weight. As a leader, are you prepared to carry the weight of this responsibility and the weight of the people you are called to serve emotionally, spiritually, physically, and mentally? What does the weight of this role look like? Let's unpack this.

Handling the Weight

As worshippers who lead, carrying the weight looks like *valuing people.* My pastor often says, "People are not just resources but answers to prayers." The people who God allows us to serve belong to Him and we serve Him by serving them. Are you emotionally, spiritually, physically, and mentally prepared to value His people? Jesus gives us an example to follow in Matthew 20:28 (KJV), which says, *"The Son of Man came not to be served but to serve others."* Knowing how to handle the weight of God's people is important. Value them beyond a Planning Center schedule or assignment. Handling the weight is seeing them as God sees them. It's being watchful and prayerful for their lives. It's being attentive to their growth in the church and out. I found that my influence in the lives of the ones God called me to serve happened more off the stage than on the stage. I often tell my team I'm doing life with them because it is true. We lead people back to the cross. We help them to identify and connect how living a life of worship directly impacts their everyday walking around life. That takes you as a leader intentionally pouring wisdom and knowledge from your own experiences. It's seeing people through their worst moments, best moments, inconsistent moments, committed moments, etc. That's why being spiritually, mentally, physically, and emotionally prepared is important.

Foundational Truth:
When we understand the weight, we can appropriately value the people.

18

Another aspect of handling the weight is understanding the value of the connection between the Pastor and the Worship Leader. We are people of authority under authority. We are servant leaders. We've heard for many years that as the head goes, the body goes. Our pastors have been given the responsibility of vision, and our role is to follow them as they follow Christ. So that means praying for our pastors, submitting to our pastors, speaking well of our pastors, and giving to our pastors.

The relationship between the Pastor and the Worship Leader is crucial. How you submit to authority will directly reflect how people submit to you. That does not mean that you will always agree with decisions that are made; however, spiritual maturity will cause you to keep your ear attentive to God. In your obedience to Him, He will cause the alignment of hearts on all matters.

Pause Moment:

What personal experiences do you believe can benefit those you serve? Write a prayer for those you have been called to serve and a prayer for your Pastors.

_____

_____

_____

_____

_____

_____

_____

_____

_____

_____

_____

_____

_____

_____

Worship as a lifestyle is a transformative journey. Embrace it fully, allowing it to shape every aspect of your life. As you continue on this path, you will discover a deeper, more fulfilling relationship with God, and your life will become a testament to His grace and glory.

Chapter 3 - Position vs. Calling

As a worship leader, we take on many roles, such as teacher, preacher, intercessor, coach and encourager; just to name a few. It's important to understand that this is a calling, not just a position. A calling or purpose is who you are, it's who you are no matter what. A position, however, is interchangeable; it is a temporary responsibility based on skill and function. My purpose as an encourager is who I am, no matter the position. As a worship leader, I must understand that as scripture says, I become all things to all people, that I might win some. My calling as a worship leader can be called upon at any moment, depending on the need. I am a servant leader at the core.

I love how Romans 12:8 speaks: *If your gift is to encourage others, BE encouraging. If it is giving, give generously. If God has given you leadership ability, take the responsibility seriously.* It goes on to say, *"This is our reasonable service and our spiritual worship to God."* (AMP)

Therefore, the title doesn't define me, but my purpose and God's words define me. I must be willing to yield to all the various gifts in me as God calls upon them. I also need to be honest with myself and others when I am weak in an area or need assistance. God has put people in our lives to aid in the movement of the vision (Ephesians 4:11-16).

I can hold a position, but it doesn't mean it's my calling! When you have a calling for something, you have a burden for it. You think about it often, dream about it, have constant thoughts of how to make it better, and always seek solutions and growth. You don't clock out of it. It's a 24-hour affection. A calling is not just a hobby or a status symbol; it's a lifelong commitment. Understanding the value of being an instrument and the power of being used by God is crucial. Imagine an instrument in a room playing itself - it would be considered strange, right? Well, we are like vessels, capable of both honor and dishonor, but the true power of the instrument is realized when someone picks it up, uses it, and brings it to life. It"s essential to recognize the value of being an instrument, being called, being chosen, and being used by God. When we try to put ourselves at the forefront instead of allowing ourselves to be used by God, we are not at our best. We come alive when God breathes life into us - we are His instruments. Strive for excellence, integrity, and purpose in all you do, recognizing that your vocation is a calling to honor God and serve others.

Pause Moment:

What's your personal why?

_____

_____

_____

_____

_____

_____

_____

_____

_____

_____

_____

_____

_____

_____

_____

Chapter 4 - Intentional Leadership

S o far on our journey, we have come to realize that through reflection, we can see that God has been preparing us for this calling. We understand that worship is not just the lifting of our hands, but it's the submission of our hearts to God. Living a life of worship is a sacrifice, and it's weighty. We've learned that as instruments, we have been entrusted to serve well, lead well, and value people, all the while submitting to the authority of God and our leaders. Knowing that if we are called, then we are equipped.

So, where do we continue? We continue by being intentional. As mentioned in a previous chapter, there will be expectations placed on you as a result of accepting this call. However, don't fret. Remember you have been equipped, and being intentional will aid in setting the proper standards. One way worship leaders demonstrate intentionality is by being prepared. My pastor often says Leaders show up first! Well, how does that live? What does it look like to be intentional? It's preparation. It's setting a consistent expectation of vision, stability, openness, and trust with your team. That can look like being the first face they see at rehearsals and Sunday morning report time. It's sending out music ahead of time so that the team has time to study and pray. It's proper planning of events, rehearsals, outings, sermon series, and meetings on a calendar for your team. It's delegating roles and setting proper expectations of those roles. It sounds simple, but being intentional in these areas breeds a healthy culture and sets an atmosphere for worship leaders and members to grow together. My pastor often says, "Healthy people make a healthy sound." It's true! Being intentional in everything creates a creative and purposeful culture. How often are you vision casting, setting expectations, and reminding your team of the why? One of the values in our ministry is, "We ask Why, because where purpose is unknown abuse is inevitable."[1] Where there is no intentional vision and standard there will always be a default. Usually, that default is to whatever the last intentional standard was, whether good or bad. We often see pain points in ministry because there is no intentional revelation or vision from God. The Bible tells us in Proverbs 29:18, *"Where there is no vision, the people perish."* (KJV) Another translation says, *"They stumble all over themselves."* (AMP) Intentionality with the vision is vital. Write it down and make it plain so that those who read it can run with it. Habakkuk 2:2 (KJV). We don't carry the vision alone. So, we must be intentional and clear.

Pause Moment:

What are some intentional standards in your team's current culture? What new intentional standards demand your attention and protection?

_____

_____

_____

_____

_____

_____

_____

_____

_____

_____

_____

Once the vision and intentional standards are set, then alignment of areas can be addressed:

Music: Aligning with the Message

Ensuring that the music aligns with the message of your house and the sermon series is crucial. The songs chosen should reflect your community's core themes and teachings, reinforcing the message and fostering a cohesive worship experience. This intentionality bridges the gap between the preached word and the sung worship, creating a unified spiritual journey.

Questions to ask yourself:

- What is the purpose of the song?
- Who is the audience?
- What does the song mean?
- How does it connect with my life?
- What scriptures has God shown me that speak to the song?

Remember, we are talking about intentional leadership. As worship leaders, our alignment is the Holy Spirit. He is there to teach us and lead us into all truth. That's such a beautiful thing—we don't have to figure it out on our own. The Holy

Spirit will always align us with truth. That's why we must worship in spirit and in truth.

Truth alignment

The Holy Spirit's role is to lead us and guide us in intentional worship and leadership. Truth is the word of God. You would think that, as worship leaders, it would be an intentional focus, but unfortunately, that can be hidden. Often, we focus on the hype, the leap, the riffs and runs, the jump, the music, and the intensity of the lights, making the truth of God a second thought instead of the first thought. As worship leaders, we must intentionally make the main thing the main thing. With the help of the Holy Spirit's guidance, He will constantly align us with truth. Worshiping in truth is worshiping in the word.

In Colossians 3:16, the word tells us *to " Let the word of Christ dwell in you richly in all wisdom, teaching and admonishing one another in psalms and hymns and spiritual songs, singing with grace in your hearts to the Lord."* (NJKV)

This is why the songs we sing must align with truth. We are responsible for admonishing and uplifting one another. We know that 'out of our hearts flow the issues of life' and that our words have power. We are protectors of the atmosphere and shepherds to what the listeners hear. The Holy Spirit recently said to me, "Avari, you know when people enter sanctuaries, they are coming in with heart songs that they have been rehearsing for days, sometimes for months and years." He said, "These heart songs sound like 'Can I make it?', 'Is God with me?', 'Why, Lord?', 'God, I trust You, but', 'God, I need You.' They have written and sung the verses over and over again." He said, "Avari, your responsibility is **to give them the chorus or the revamp or the reprise of hope** through the songs we sing in worship." I was like wow, that is so true. Therefore, the worship songs we choose should be an intentional confession of faith. Singing songs because they are popular on the top 100 chart may be good for you but not for the body. We are responsible for the seeds and heart songs planted in the hearer. Talk about letting the word of truth dwell in us richly!

If you get a chance, read the full chapter of Ezekiel 3. Look at how God commissions Ezekiel with the responsibility of carrying the word of truth. The scripture I want to pull out is verse 10 where it says, "*Let all my words sink deep into your own heart first.*" (NJKV) Listen to them carefully for yourself, then go to the people and say them. As worship leaders, we must seek the Lord about the songs, and what we sing and even what we say in a song. Even down to our ad-libbing. Write it down, re-hearse it, be sure it aligns with truth as well.

Foundational Truth:
Lead with intentionality, alignment and truth.

Chapter 5 - Peaks and Valleys

Man, Avari you take this really seriously, you may say. I do! We have to; it matters! We have talked about how being a worship leader can be a weighty but fulfilling assignment. It presents a series of peaks and valleys, each with its unique set of challenges. But like we discovered in the beginning, when you know your why, it sustains you through it all. Seeing challenges as growth opportunities rather than problems is the first step in appropriately managing the weight. My pastor always says how you see the problem is the problem. Being adaptable and adjustable through the peaks and valleys will keep you in a posture of freedom. Peaks allow you to see where you've been, and valleys allow you to see where you are going. Both are essential parts of growth. Imagine and think about how Jesus handled peaks and valleys. All through the New Testament, we see how Jesus led the disciples in moments of praise and miracles and, at the same time, doubts, fears, confusion, etc. One thing we know

Jesus did was, regardless of the vantage point, He led with grace. Even in moments of difficulty, He led with grace. As worship leaders, we must display that same humility. How do we see Jesus leading with grace? It's seen as forgiveness, understanding, reconciliation, recompense, and offering provision in the midst of confusion. We also see leading in grace and with grace in Genesis; even after Adam and Eve sinned, God still provided for them. He gave them skin to cover themselves. He could have left them without, but he provided grace. Leading with grace is a daily practice. It may not always be comfortable, but it's important.

One of the primary challenges faced is the complex navigation of decision-making processes, making sound decisions, and effectively managing any disagreements that may arise. Before you make decisions, address your teams, or call meetings, be sure that your filter is grace. This must be a thought determined beforehand, before facing a peak or a valley.

Additionally, managing a team with varying skill levels adds another layer of complexity. Adapting to the differing skill sets within the team and gracefully handling conflicts that arise when skill levels don't align with the task requirements can be a significant challenge for the worship leader. How do you deal with those moments of conflict, with Grace?

Another important thing to remember when faced with peaks and valleys is to lead with compassion. The old saying still holds true: "People don't care how much you know until they know how much you care." Compassion should be prioritized over discipline when leading. Even when you're displeased, let compassion guide your actions. Be just as excited to praise victories. Offer praise in public and provide corrections in private. View every moment as a teachable opportunity rather than simply a chance to correct.

Keys points

- Address the problem, not the emotions.
- Don't be reactive but proactive.
- Not every objection needs a response; raise the standard.
- Make allowances for people.

In ministry, the flow of peaks and valleys is inevitable and unpredictable. As a worship leader, it is your responsibility to keep vision and standards at the forefront as you navigate with your team. Worship extends beyond personal devotion to encompass how you engage with others. Love, service, and community are integral to a worshipful life. Foster relationships that reflect Christ's love and humility, and actively seek opportunities to serve and support those around you, making each interaction a testament to your faith.

Understanding that peaks and valleys are integral to leading a worship team helps prepare leaders for the diverse experiences they will encounter. Embracing the highs with gratitude and navigating the lows with resilience creates a balanced approach to leadership.

Effective worship leaders focus on the bigger picture: nurturing a spirit of worship and fostering an environment where team members can thrive spiritually and creatively. By recognizing and appreciating the peaks, addressing the valleys with care, and remaining committed to the overarching mission of worship, leaders can guide their teams through a fulfilling and impactful journey. In this dynamic landscape, each peak and valley contribute to the richness of the worship experience, shaping not only the team but also the hearts of those they lead in worship.

Cultivating Culture is Important

In the heart of every vibrant church service lies a worship team dedicated to creating an atmosphere where congregants can connect deeply with the divine. The culture within a worship team significantly influences the spiritual and musical experiences they offer. Understanding and nurturing this culture is essential for any worship team striving to lead with authenticity, unity, and excellence.

Culture is important to your team. What is culture? Culture is the beliefs, standards, values, and ways of being in a collective group. The Culture is the blueprint that is referred to for alignment and harmony. Understanding these foundations helps shape a team's identity and practices. In the journey of peaks and valleys, a continual view of the culture should be a frequent assessment. I've learned over the years to be watchful of the team, assessing the temperature continually. "You get what you inspect, not just what you expect." At one point in our culture, the team was very inconsistent and non-committed, and excuses were over the top. So, I began to look at what was causing the breakdown. I started with the inconsistency with our gifts. People were constantly hoarse, fatigued, and taking breaks left and right. We were picking songs out of the team's range, not giving tools to help them maintain stamina or vocal strength, and just pushing and expecting them to do it without complaining. We made it a problem when someone needed a sabbatical instead of looking at what the underlying problem was, which was that we weren't paying attention to their needs. Once this was recognized, I began to change the type of songs we did, and I began to lower the keys to fit our range, giving them the confidence they needed. Within a month or two, I started to see growth. When someone talked about needing a sabbatical, I walked with them through it with the perspective below:

Questions I would pose to members taking sabbaticals:
- What is the purpose of the sabbatical?
- What are your written goals?
- What is your set return date?

Another culture shift was this: after looking at how we were using the gifts, I looked at our structure. People need structure. The book *The Perfect Day Formula* by Craig Ballantyne states, "Structures equal freedom." Being punctual, having systems, and being prepared aids in the cultivation of the culture.[2] Once we started having planned rehearsals, weekly updates, punctual rehearsals, Sunday morning prayers, and sending songs out prior to rehearsal (months in advance) with correct keys and vocal breakdowns, it created freedom and security within the team. Now a true expectation can be given. Cultivating a worship team culture is an ongoing journey that requires dedication, reflection, and adaptation.

Chapter 6 - Leading Worship: Skills and Techniques

L eading worship effectively requires a blend of spiritual sensitivity, practical skills, and a deep understanding of your congregation. Here's a deeper dive into some essential aspects:

1. Effective Communication and Engagement

Engaging with your congregation goes beyond just singing songs. It involves creating an atmosphere where worshippers feel connected and involved. Start by understanding your congregation's needs and expectations. Tailor your communication style to be genuine and approachable. Use storytelling, scripture, and personal reflections to bridge the gap between the worship team and the congregation.

2. Navigating Transitions and Flow

Smooth transitions between songs and service elements help maintain the worship experience's momentum. Plan your transitions thoughtfully. Practice changes in tempo, key, or mood to ensure they feel seamless. Consider the flow of the service and how each component leads naturally into the next.

3. Enhancing Congregational Participation

Encourage participation by choosing songs and elements that resonate with the congregation. Provide clear, supportive leadership during the service to guide the congregation. Use visual aids or handouts if necessary to help people follow along, especially if introducing new songs or liturgies.

Leading worship is both a privilege and a responsibility. It's about guiding others in expressing their faith and connecting with God in a meaningful way. By combining spiritual insight with practical skills, you can create worship experiences that inspire and transform.

Chapter 7 - Practical Tips

No guide would be complete without a handy list of tips. Here are a few forged in the fire of my experiences:

Tip#1: Leaders should have quarterly or yearly assessments with each of their team members.

I created a 6-C's questionnaire template to use during these meetings:

1. **Care:** Ask the member, "How is your personal life? Do you have any updates?"
2. **Clarity:** As a member, what is your understanding of the vision and mission, and what does it mean to you?
3. **Connectivity:** How do you see yourself growing and expanding within the vision, and are there any growth opportunities?
4. **Correc**t/Expectation: As the leader, address any areas and/or habits the member is doing that need to stop and those that need to continue. (Gain clarity)
5. **Challenge:** Challenge members with a directive, goal, and growth opportunity.

6. **Compassion:** Leave the session with speaking encouragement and empowerment.

Tip #2. Be sure to keep an updated version of the church calendar accessible. Plan songs and rehearsals at least one month ahead of each major event. Start planning summer events in January and Christmas/New Year's events in mid-July or August.

Tip#3. Create a team to assist you and meet with them frequently. Don't do it all on your own. Here's a starter list of team members needed:

- **Wardrobe**: responsible for creating the monthly attire board
- **Assistant**: responsible for organizing the rosters, and calendars
- **Song set**: responsible for choosing the song sets for the week or month
- **Core leadership**: coaches that lead groups, carry the vision

Tip #4. Effective communication and collaboration are cornerstones of a healthy worship team culture. Communication forms include:

a. Email
b. Text line
c. Band app
d. Planning Center

Tip #5. Create rotation schedules for your teams.

A rotation schedule is essential for preventing team burnout and ensuring that team members have time to be fed spiritually and emotionally. It allows members to step back from their responsibilities periodically, preventing fatigue and ensuring that they have the opportunity to rest and recharge. By rotating responsibilities, team members can maintain a healthy balance between serving others and being nourished themselves, ultimately leading to a more sustainable and fulfilling experience for everyone involved.

Chapter 8 - Conclusion-Embracing the Journey

As our exploration into leading worship concludes, it is fitting to reflect on the journey we have shared. We began with the foundational elements of worship leadership, delving into the art of reflecting and the art of aligning our hearts with God. We explored the heart of a worship leader, the importance of authenticity, and the intricate dance of guiding a congregation through moments of deep connection and profound reverence. Leading worship is not merely a role but a calling—a sacred invitation to facilitate encounters with the Father and to shepherd a community in its spiritual journey. This calling is multifaceted, demanding creativity, empathy, and resilience. It requires a balance of passion and patience, innovation and tradition, guidance and freedom.

As we've navigated these elements together, it's become clear that the essence of worship leadership lies in a continual process of growth and reflection. One of the most profound truths about leading worship is that it is a journey with no definitive endpoint. Each worship service is both a culmination and a new beginning. The songs, prayers, and rituals we use are not static formulas but dynamic expressions that evolve with each gathering.

As you move forward in your journey, remember that every service is an opportunity to deepen your connection with the community you serve and to explore new dimensions of faith. In reflecting on your role, consider the following guiding principles:

1. Cultivate a Heart of Service: At its core, worship leadership is about service. It's about creating spaces where people can encounter God and be transformed. Approach your role with humility and a willingness to serve, not just in the moments of public worship but also in your everyday interactions with your community.

2. Embrace Continuous Learning: The landscape of worship is ever-changing, influenced by cultural shifts, technological advancements, and evolving congregational needs. Stay open to learning and growing, whether through formal education, mentorship, or personal reflection. The most effective worship leaders are those who remain curious and adaptable.

3. Foster Community and Connection: Worship is a communal activity that thrives on relationships. Invest time in building connections within your team and understanding their needs and spiritual experiences. Create environments where everyone feels valued and heard, and where genuine relationships can flourish.

4. Balance Tradition and Innovation: While it's important to honor the traditions and liturgies that shape your worship practices, be open to exploring new forms and expressions. Innovation can breathe new life into worship, but it should always serve the purpose of deepening spiritual engagement and community connection.

5. Nurture Your Spiritual Life: Your own spiritual health is crucial to your effectiveness as a worship leader. Prioritize personal time for prayer, reflection, and spiritual growth. Your own journey of faith will profoundly impact your ability to lead others.

6. Seek Support and Accountability: No one leads in isolation. Surround yourself with a supportive team, mentors, and peers who can offer guidance, encouragement, and constructive feedback. Mutual support and accountability are key to sustaining a vibrant and healthy worship ministry.

As you step into the next chapter of your journey, remember that leading worship is both a privilege and a responsibility. It is a calling that demands your heart, your creativity, and your commitment. Trust in the process, and be confident in the unique gifts and perspectives you bring to your role. The journey of worship leadership is both challenging and rewarding, filled with moments of joy, growth, and transformation. Embrace it with an open heart and a spirit of gratitude. As you continue to lead, may you find inspiration in every worship experience, and may your leadership foster a deeper sense of connection and devotion within your community.

Thank you for allowing me to accompany you on this journey. May your path be blessed, your leadership be impactful, and your heart remain ever open to the grace and wonder of worship!

Notes

1. Munroe, Myles. *Understanding the Purpose and Power of Woman*. Whitaker House, 2001.

2. Ballantyne, Craig. *The Perfect Day Formula: How to Own the Day and Control Your Life*. Early to Rise Publishing, 2015.

3. The Holy Bible: Amplified Version. (AMP) The Lockman Foundation, 1987, 2015.

4. The Holy Bible: King James Version (KJV). Oxford UP, 1769.

5. The Holy Bible: The Message (MSG). NavPress, 2002.

6. The Holy Bible: New King James Version (NKJV). Thomas Nelson, 1982.

About the Author

Avari's stylish jazzy, pop sound is designed to uplift listeners above the daily cares of life. A gifted songwriter, singer, worshipper and recording artist, Avari writes inspiring lyrics and sings music that encourages listeners to look beyond their present reality to focus on the real meaning of life found only in Christ.

Born and raised in Tampa, Florida, Avari was extremely shy and quiet as a child. Yet, she knew something was different about her. She started singing at the same time she began talking. Early on, Avari discovered the unique, powerful gift of her voice. Avari's love for the gift God had given her began when she was asked to sing at her pastor's appreciation event.

In 2003, God spoke to Avari about using her gift to be a voice for young ladies and men across the world. At that moment, Avari abandoned her plans of becoming a pediatrician to dedicate her gifts to God's glory. In 2005, Avari was asked to join a new local recording label called Sound Right Productions. On this platform, she began to release her gift to the world. Avari realized the beauty of her music as part of the 7-member group True, which released four records.

In 2007, Avari released her first solo project entitled "Love Destroys the Pain." In 2010, God opened the door for Avari to be the praise and worship leader of her church, Revealing Truth Ministries. Since that time, Avari has used her gift in Florida, Memphis, Atlanta, Texas and Virginia. She also has written theme songs for the ITWorks Company and the Go Green campaign. She has appeared on stage with great musicians, including Gammage, Lisa McClendon, Canton Jones, Mr. Del, Da Truth, and Pee Wee Callins. In 2018, she released her second solo project entitled "Mahogany Doors". The door continued to be opened which allowed her to write and be featured on two albums from Revealing Truth Ministries as well as various theme songs and conference anthems. Avari has been featured on various projects with locals around the Tampa Bay area and to work with top producers such as Shorne "2SC" Callahan. She has had the great opportunity of singing the National Anthem at several events such as the Thaddeus Bullards campaign "Walk of Love", The Buccaneers pre-games, Graduation ceremonies, and The Stomp Down experience.

Avari discovered her passion of connecting with people through the message of hope through music. In Christ, Avari found her only hope for enduring the challenges of life and overcoming insecurities, the fear of failure and abuse.

Through her music, Avari aspires to reach generations across the world by helping people to see hope beyond present circumstances, knowing God's love is the answer to every problem.

Avari desires to be a figure of hope, light and encouragement in life and through music. She knows God has a great calling on her life to spread the good news of God's love across the world. Through her obedience to Jesus Christ and His message delivered through her, Avari believes people will be forever changed!